W9-BME-117

DATE DUE

DEMCO 38-297

SOCCER
FOR FUN!

By Kenn Goin

Content Adviser: Richard Landon, Youth Soccer Coach, New Haven, Connecticut
Reading Adviser: Frances J. Bonacci, Reading Specialist, Cambridge, Massachusetts

COMPASS POINT BOOKS

MINNEAPOLIS, MINNESOTA

Compass Point Books
3109 West 50th Street, #115
Minneapolis, MN 55410

Visit Compass Point Books on the Internet at *www.compasspointbooks.com*
or e-mail your request to *custserv@compasspointbooks.com*

Editors: Ryan Blitstein/Bill SMITH STUDIO and Catherine Neitge
Photo Researchers: Christie Silver and Sandra Will/Bill SMITH STUDIO
Designer: Jay Jaffe/Bill SMITH STUDIO

Library of Congress Cataloging-in-Publication Data
Goin, Kenn.
    Soccer for fun! / by Kenn Goin.
       p. cm. — (Sports for fun)
    Summary: Describes the basic rules, skills, and important people and events in the sport of soccer.
    Includes bibliographical references (p.) and index.
    ISBN 0-7565-0431-7
    1. Soccer—Juvenile literature. [1. Soccer.] I. Title. II. Series.
    GV943.25 .G58 2003
    796.334—dc21   2002015122

Table of Contents

Note: In this book, there are two kinds of vocabulary words. Soccer Words to Know are words specific to soccer. They are in **bold** and are defined on page 46. Other Words to Know are helpful words that aren't related only to soccer. They are in ***bold and italicized***. These are defined on page 47.

The Beautiful Game

Soccer is the most popular team sport in the world. People of all ages play soccer. You don't have to be big to be a good soccer player. In fact, some of the best soccer players in the world are small. Soccer players zigzag down the field. Sometimes they flip themselves in the air before kicking the ball.

Get Your Goals

The object of the game is to get the ball into the opponent's goal to score a point. Only one player, the goalkeeper, can use his or her hands. All other players use their feet, knees, and (sometimes) their heads to control the ball. Teams can steal the ball from each other at any time during play. Soccer is an exciting, *unpredictable* game!

The number 5 soccer ball is used by professionals. It is about 27 inches (71 cm) around and weighs about 13 ounces (397 g). The number 4 ball, for 7–12 year olds, weighs 12 ounces (340 g).

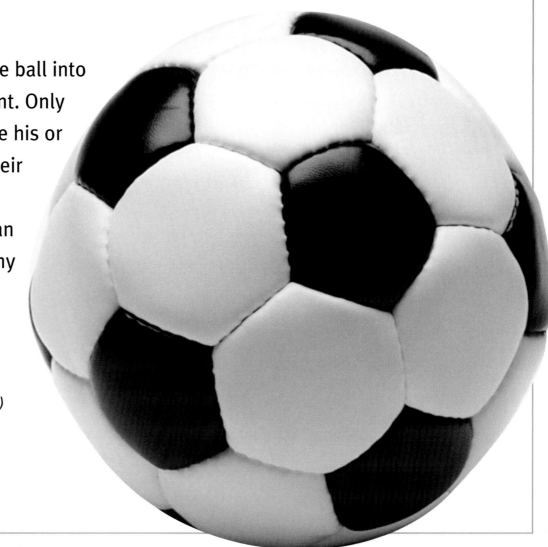

Where to Kick It

While the fields in most sports must all be one size, soccer fields *vary*. They may be as long as 130 yards (120 m) and as wide as 100 yards (90 m). The important thing is that the field is always *rectangular*. Look at the picture to learn the names of the parts of the soccer field.

center circle

center line

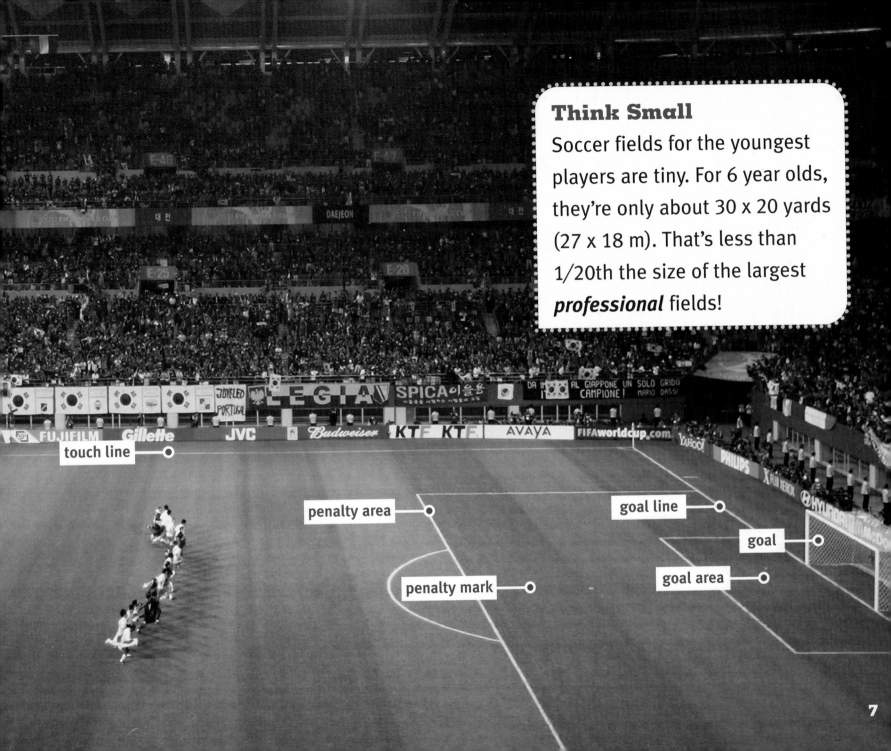

Think Small

Soccer fields for the youngest players are tiny. For 6 year olds, they're only about 30 x 20 yards (27 x 18 m). That's less than 1/20th the size of the largest *professional* fields!

touch line

penalty area

goal line

goal

penalty mark

goal area

7

Go For the Goal!

There's only one way to score points in soccer. Get the ball over the opponent's goal line, between the posts, and under the crossbar. Goals are usually shot with the **instep**, the inside of the foot. When a player is near the goal and a teammate passes the ball at foot level, the player can whack the ball into the goal with the instep. This scoring play is called a **volley**. If the ball bounces once after the pass, it's called a **half-volley**.

*One of the coolest-looking ways to score is the **bicycle kick**. In this dangerous move, a player jumps into the air, kicking back as if pedaling a bicycle.*

Scoring Strategies

- Take shots quickly. Don't wait for the perfect setup.

- Don't aim for the goalkeeper (see p. 16). Aim for the edges of the goal.

- Keep an eye on the ball after the shot. If it rebounds, kick it back into the goal.

What to Wear

Soccer players are fast movers. They need comfortable, lightweight clothes and safety gear.

Shoes are the most important piece of equipment. They are usually made of soft, *flexible* leather. This allows players to feel the ball when their feet touch it. The shoes have cleats on the bottom. Plastic cleats help players stop and turn quickly on the field.

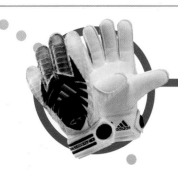

Goalie Gear

Because they use their hands, goalkeepers need soft, flexible gloves. They are often made of *latex*, so it's easier to grip the ball.

Jerseys, or shirts, are long-sleeved in fall and winter. They are short-sleeved in spring and summer, or when playing indoor games. Loose shorts that allow freedom of movement are best. In chilly or wet weather, tracksuits can be helpful, too.

Plastic or rubberlike shin pads protect the lower legs against scrapes and bruises. They must be completely covered by socks.

Start at the Center

Before the game begins, the official tosses a coin. The team that wins the toss decides which goal it will attack. The other team gets to kick the ball first. In the second half of the game, things switch. The toss winner kicks first, and the teams change the goals they defend.

After the toss, the ball is placed in the field's center circle. The two teams face each other on opposite sides of the center line. The **defensive** team (the one without the ball) must stay out of the center circle until the ball is touched by an opposing player. The **offensive** team can have a few players near the ball. The game begins when the referee blows the whistle. After the first kick, another player must touch the ball before the kicker can touch it again.

When is the Kickoff?
Kickoffs happen at the start of the game, at the beginning of the second half, and after each goal.

Moving Forward

Each team has ten **position** players and one **goalkeeper**.

There are two kinds of offensive positions:

- **Forward:** The forwards, or attackers, are the players trying to score for their team. The center forward, called a **striker**, scores about one goal per game.

- **Midfielder:** The midfielders, or halfbacks, must help defenders guard the goal. They also help forwards move the ball toward the opponent's goal. They do a lot of running up and down the field, so midfielders have to be in great shape!

Both offensive and defensive players can score at any time.

Lucky Numbers

So everyone knows who's who, different positions wear different numbers.

DEFENDERS	2-5
MIDFIELDERS	6-8
FORWARDS	9-11
GOALKEEPERS	1, 0, 00

What's a Goalkeeper?

There are two kinds of defensive positions:

- **Goalkeeper:** The goalkeeper, or "goalie," has to stop the ball from going into the net. The goalie can touch the ball with his or her hands, but only while within the penalty area. Once the ball is in hand, it must be thrown or kicked within six seconds. If it is held longer, the other team gets to take an indirect kick (see p. 34).

- **Defender**. The defender's main job is to help the goalie protect the team's goal. Sometimes, each defender has to guard one player on the other team. This is called **man-to-man** defense. Other times, defenders guard an area of the field, called a **zone**.

Hands Off!

After the ball leaves the goalkeeper's hands, he or she cannot touch it again until another player has made contact with it.

Take Control

What do players do when the ball is in front of them? They **dribble** it. Dribbling is controlling the ball with gentle taps while running. A player can use both sides—as well as the top and bottom—of the foot to dribble. This skill is one of the most important in the sport. The best players practice it every day.

Play Keep Away

Here are some tricks players use to keep opponents from taking the ball while they're dribbling:

• A player **shields** the ball by putting the body between it and the defender.

• While heading down the field, players quickly stop the ball, turn, and dribble in another direction—even if it's back toward their own goal.

• Players **fake out** the opponent by pretending to move in one direction when they're actually going to go in another. They move their head to the side, or look the other way.

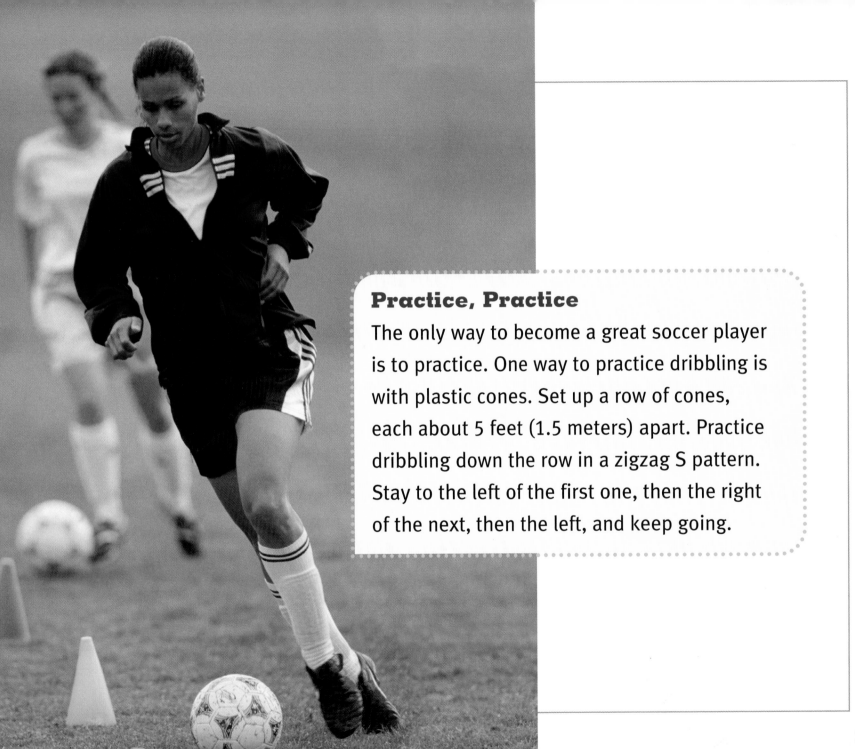

Practice, Practice

The only way to become a great soccer player is to practice. One way to practice dribbling is with plastic cones. Set up a row of cones, each about 5 feet (1.5 meters) apart. Practice dribbling down the row in a zigzag S pattern. Stay to the left of the first one, then the right of the next, then the left, and keep going.

Back and Forth

Passing the ball between players is the best way for a team to move the ball toward the goal. The basic pass is easy. Practice it before trying any of the others.

1. Plant one foot onto the ground. Point it in the direction the ball will move.

2. With the other foot, quickly kick into the ball.

3. Follow the kick through toward a teammate.

Fancy footwork while dribbling and passing helps players get past defenders.

Push It!

For short passes, use the inside of the foot to do a **push pass**. Plant the nonkicking foot next to the ball. Point it in the direction the ball will go. Turn the kicking foot so that when it swings, the inside of the foot will hit the ball in the middle. The knee should not be bent. The hip joint is what swings.

Pass It Along

After learning the basics, it's time to start practicing more complicated passes.

Heel Pass

To pass the ball to a teammate who is behind them, players hit the ball in its center with the heel. They make sure to watch as they kick, or the other team might steal the ball away.

Outside Foot Pass

The outside foot pass is great for a quick, short pass. Instead of the instep, this pass uses the outside part of the foot. Make sure to kick the top part of the ball so it doesn't go too high in the air.

Shoelace Pass

The **shoelace pass** moves the ball really far or very high into the air. Players plant the nonkicking foot as for a push pass. Then they swing the other leg forward, toe pointed down, and kick the ball with the instep. To keep the ball closer to the ground, they kick with the knee over it. To kick it higher, they plant the nonkicking foot farther from the ball (about ten inches [twenty-five cm]) and lean back a little as the kicking foot hits it.

23

Catching With Feet?

How do players get a ball that is flying their way under control? They can't catch it, but they can **trap** it! Lift one foot just off the ground so that it meets the ball halfway up its side. When the ball hits, let the foot move back a little in the direction the ball is moving. Otherwise, the ball will bounce away as if it smacked into a wall. If the ball comes high off the ground, trap it with the thigh or chest instead of the foot. Remember, players can use any part of the leg!

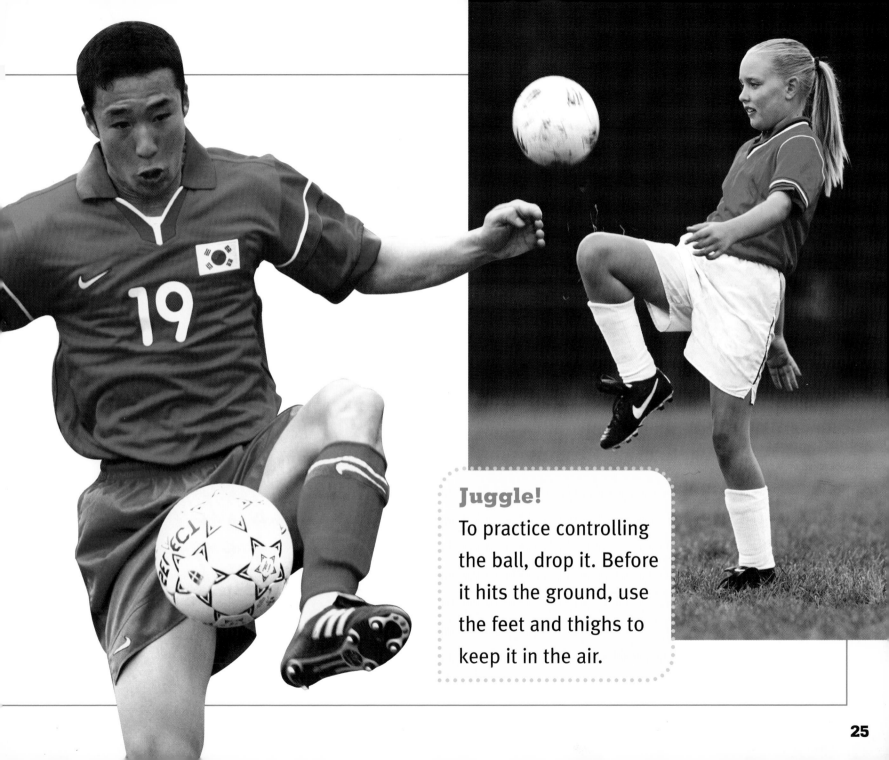

Juggle!

To practice controlling the ball, drop it. Before it hits the ground, use the feet and thighs to keep it in the air.

Using Your Head (and Chest)

They're a little bit tougher than foot trapping, but head and chest trapping can come in handy during a close game.

Head Trapping

One of the most exciting soccer moves is head trapping, or **heading**. Usually, many players jump to head the ball at the same time. Be careful not to bump heads!

How to head a ball:

• Jump up to meet the ball.

• Keep the mouth closed and eyes open.

• Hit the ball with the forehead.

In fact, studies are being done on the safety of headers. Only head trap in a game after practicing with a coach.

Chest Trapping

Players can use their chest to trap, too. They cushion the ball as it hits the chest by leaning back a little bit. Using the arms helps balance. As the ball hits them, they lean forward to drop the ball at their feet.

Over the Line

When a ball goes over a touchline, it is **out of bounds**. The last team that didn't touch the ball gets to do a **throw-in**.

How to throw-in:

- Stand outside the touchline.

- Both hands must come from behind the head and all the way over during the throw.

- The player's body must face the direction in which the ball is thrown. Both feet must be on the ground.

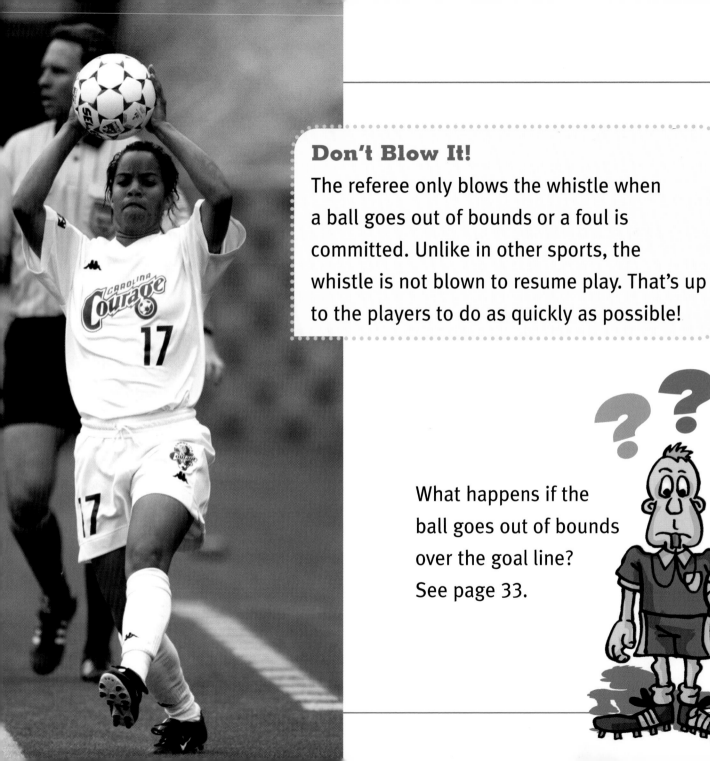

Don't Blow It!

The referee only blows the whistle when a ball goes out of bounds or a foul is committed. Unlike in other sports, the whistle is not blown to resume play. That's up to the players to do as quickly as possible!

What happens if the ball goes out of bounds over the goal line? See page 33.

Follow the Rules

Soccer is a simple game, but it has a lot of rules. Game times and **stoppage time** are basic rules. The offside rule is one of the most important rules of the game.

Game Times

Unlike football and basketball games, soccer matches usually last no more than two hours. Professional games are ninety minutes long. There is an intermission between the two forty-five-minute halves. Sometimes, in games with older players, the referee adds time to each half. This extra time is called stoppage time. It makes up for playing time missed because a player was injured, or when players came off the bench during the game.

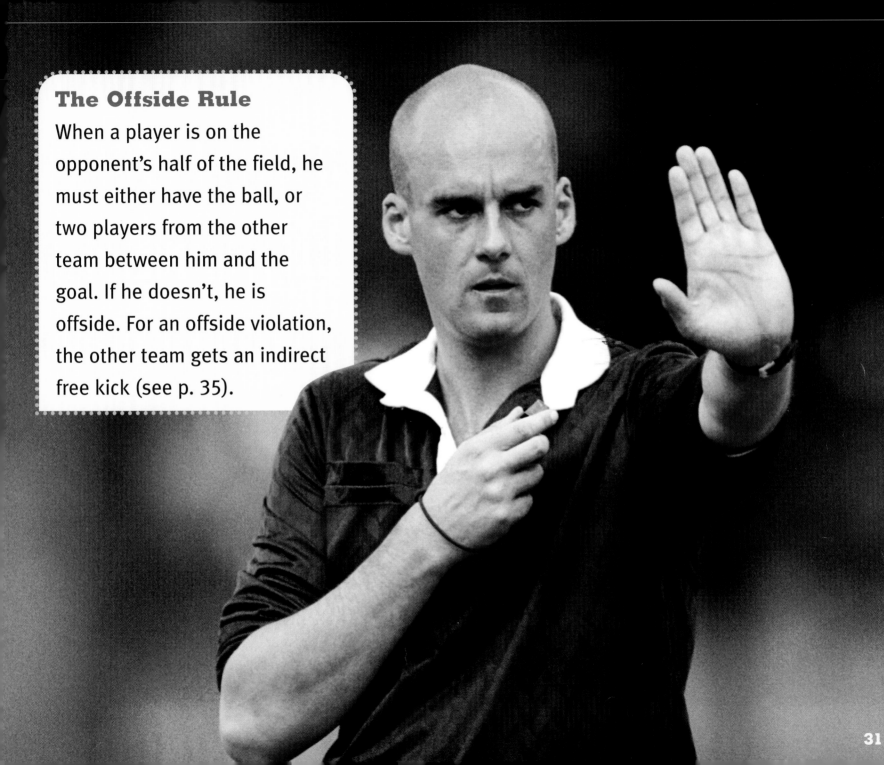

The Offside Rule

When a player is on the opponent's half of the field, he must either have the ball, or two players from the other team between him and the goal. If he doesn't, he is offside. For an offside violation, the other team gets an indirect free kick (see p. 35).

Kick Free

When a player breaks a rule during play, the referee blows the whistle and play stops. The other team is given a **free kick**. For serious rule violations, the team gets a **direct kick**. That means a player can kick directly toward the goal without the ball being touched by another player. For less serious violations, an **indirect kick** is awarded. This means the ball must be touched by another player before it can be kicked into the goal.

During penalty kicks, goalies have to play a guessing game. The ball moves so fast, the goalie has to start diving to one side of the goal before the ball is even kicked!

Here are three important kinds of free kicks:

Goal kick: When the attacking team kicks the ball over the goal line, the other team gets to kick the ball from its goal box.

Penalty kick: If a team commits a foul inside its own penalty area, the other team gets to kick the ball from the penalty spot.

Corner kick: If a team kicks the ball over its own goal line, the other team kicks the ball back into play from the field's corner.

When making a corner kick, a player kicks the ball high into the air in the goal area. If she's lucky, one of her teammates might be able to head it into the goal.

Foul!

Here are the kinds of kick awarded for each foul.

FOULS WITH DIRECT-KICK PENALTIES	FOULS WITH INDIRECT-KICK PENALTIES
Charging	Dangerous play
Handling ball	Goalkeeper offenses
Hitting	*Interfering* with goalkeeper
Holding	Blocking
Kicking	*Violation* of offside rule
Pushing	Bad conduct
Tripping	

Before an indirect kick, players from both teams line up. The offense tries to turn the ball around and into the goal. Defensive players try to kick the ball as far from the goal as possible. Sometimes things get confusing, and the ball is tapped into the goal!

You're In Trouble Now!

When one player acts badly or **repeatedly** commits fouls, a referee holds up a yellow card as a warning. If the player continues the behavior, the referee holds up a red card. That means the player is out of the game! Violence, spitting, swearing, and certain other offenses get red cards.

35

What Now?

Soccer is about more than just dribbling, passing, and kicking. The best players can think on their feet while running down the field. Here are some ideas for plays.

• It's OK to pass a ball backwards on the field. Sometimes players have to pass the ball back toward their own goal to get around the other team.

• Switching the ball from one side of the field to the other is a good idea. It keeps the other team on the move.

• Make sure teammates are open before passing them the ball. A bad pass could mean a goal for the other team!

Up Against the Wall

Sometimes, a player uses a **wall pass** to get around the defense. She passes the ball to a teammate, and the defender runs after it. The player runs away quickly. Then, when she's in the clear, her teammate passes the ball back to her.

Legends

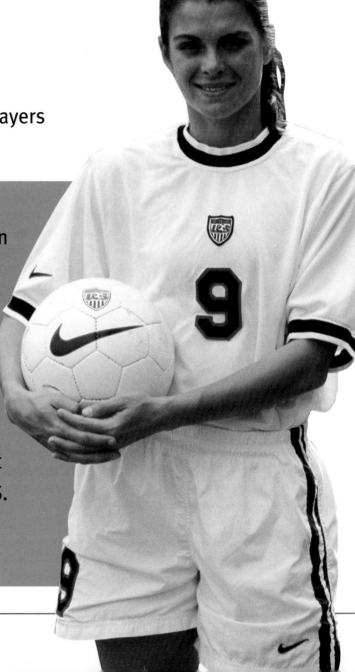

There are thousands of great soccer players all over the world. These two are stars!

Mia Hamm

Mia Hamm is the most famous American woman to play soccer. She was born in 1972 in Selma, Alabama. She is probably the best female player in the world today. Hamm is the all-time women's international scoring leader with 115 goals. She's a great forward who first played on the national level at age fifteen. In 1999, she helped the U.S. National team win the Women's World Cup title.

Pelé

Many people believe Pelé is the greatest soccer player of all time. He was born Edson Arantes do Nascimento in Brazil in 1940. *Time* magazine named him one of the twenty "Heroes and Icons" of the 20th century. At seventeen, Pelé helped Brazil win a World Cup championship game. He went on to help win two additional World Cup titles in the next twelve years. Pelé is the only player so far to perform on three world championship teams. He is the second-highest goal scorer of all time, with over 1,200 goals. (Artur Friedenreich is the highest with 1,329 goals.) In 1975, Pelé moved to the United States to play for the New York Cosmos. This helped launch the youth soccer movement in the U.S.

Bobby Moore (far right) of England exchanges jerseys with Pelé after a 1970 World Cup match.

The Big Match

The World Cup certainly has the right name. It is one of the biggest sporting events in the entire world. Teams from hundreds of nations compete in the tournament. It takes place once every four years.

The World Cup was created in 1928 by Jules Rimet. He was president of the soccer world's governing body, the *Federation Internationale de Football Association* (FIFA). The first World Cup took place in Uruguay in 1930. The first Women's World Cup took place in 1991 in China.

More than five billion people watch the final match on television. Celebrations take place in the streets in many of the countries before, during, and after games. Some fans get up in the middle of the night to watch their country's team play on TV. It's an exciting time for soccer fans around the world.

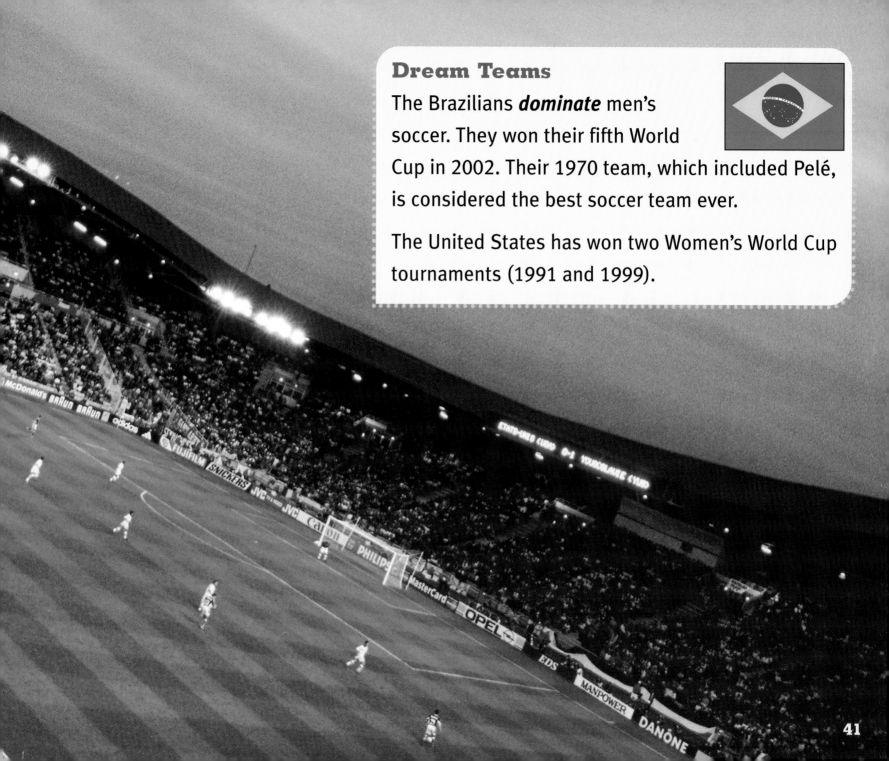

Dream Teams

The Brazilians **dominate** men's soccer. They won their fifth World Cup in 2002. Their 1970 team, which included Pelé, is considered the best soccer team ever.

The United States has won two Women's World Cup tournaments (1991 and 1999).

What Happened When?

1500 B.C. **1609** **1860** **1870** **1900** **1910** **1920** **1930**

1500 B.C. The earliest known version of soccer is played in China.

1609 A form of soccer is played in Jamestown, Virginia.

1863 First "Laws of the Game" are approved by the London Football Association.

1872 The world's oldest soccer tournament, the English FA, is formed.

1904 Soccer is organized on a world scale when FIFA is formed by seven European countries.

1914 The National Challenge Cup, the first national U.S. soccer tournament, is established.

1930 The first World Cup is played.

Uruguay won the 1930 World Cup. ▶

42

40   **1950**   **1960**   **1970**   **1980**   **1990**   **2000**

1938 Numbers are used for the first time on players' shirts in the World Cup.

1956-1960 The Spanish team Real Madrid wins five consecutive European Cups.

1966 England's Geoff Hurst scores the most discussed goal in World Cup history when he kicks the ball into the crossbar and over the goal line.

1972 As a result of Title IX, a change to education laws that gave female athletes equal rights, hundreds of U.S. colleges form women's soccer teams.

1975 Pelé moves to the United States.

1996 Major League Soccer (MLS), the most popular U.S. soccer league, plays its first season.

1999 U.S. team wins the Women's World Cup.

2001 The number of American girls playing high school soccer reaches 270,000.

43

Stupendous Soccer Facts

England in the 1800s had two kinds of football: rugby and association football (based on FIFA rules). People called association football assoc football. Since America already had another kind of football, the name **assoc football** was shortened to soccer in the U.S.!

Soccer is *futbol* in Spanish, *fussball* in German, and *aqsaqtuk* in Inuit!

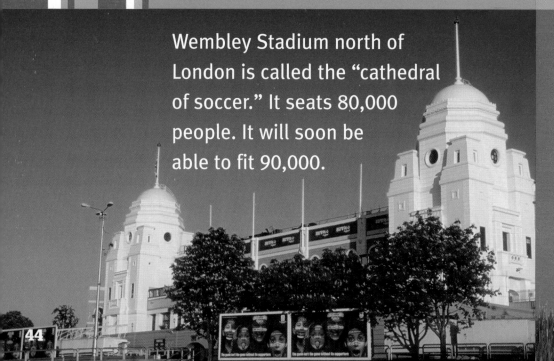

Wembley Stadium north of London is called the "cathedral of soccer." It seats 80,000 people. It will soon be able to fit 90,000.

Close to four million children play soccer in the U.S. Youth Soccer League. Memberships are growing at a rate of 200,000 new players every year!

After the 1970 World Soccer Cup game between El Salvador and Honduras, the countries fought a three-day war!

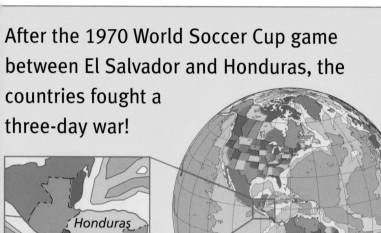

Honduras

El Salvador

After matches, players often trade shirts. This tradition may have started at the 1954 World Cup in Switzerland.

When Giuseppe Meazza of Italy made a penalty kick in a 1938 World Cup game, his shorts fell down! The elastic had been torn earlier in the match. Before the kick, he'd been holding them up with one hand.

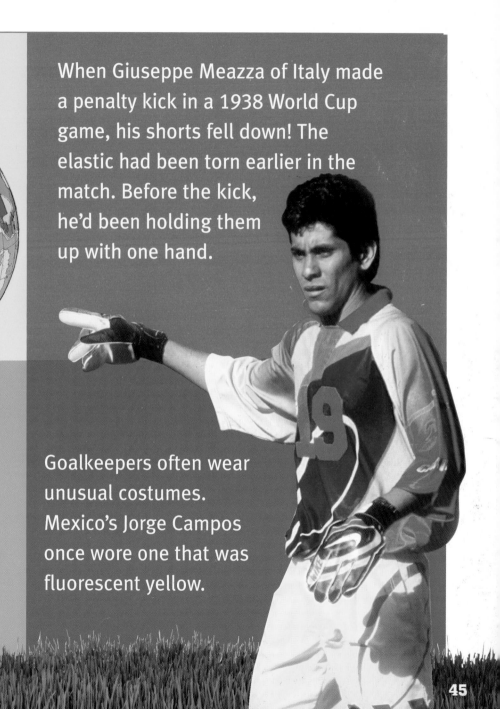

Goalkeepers often wear unusual costumes. Mexico's Jorge Campos once wore one that was fluorescent yellow.

Soccer Words to Know

center circle: the circle in the middle of the playing field used for the kickoff

center line: the line drawn across the middle of the playing field

corner kick: a kick from a corner of the field; awarded to a team when its opponents kick the ball over the goal line

direct kick: a kind of free kick; the player can kick directly at the goal without the ball being kicked to another teammate first

dribbling: a way for a player to control the ball as he or she moves down the field

FIFA: the Federation Internationale de Football Association; international soccer association that issues rules for the game

foul: a violation of a rule

free kick: a kick given to a team because the other team committed a foul or made a goal

goal: a point scored; also the netted area into which the ball must fall for a goal to be scored

goal area: the rectangular area immediately in front of the goal

goal kick: a kind of free kick awarded to a team when the other team has kicked the ball over the goal line

half-volley: a kick to a ball that has bounced once

indirect kick: a kind of free kick in which the ball must be kicked by more than one player before it can be kicked at the goal

instep: the top part of the foot

juggling: repeatedly using the feet, thighs or head to keep the ball in the air without letting it touch the ground.

kickoff: a kind of kick from the center circle used to start games, the second halves of games, and after a goal has been scored

penalty area: the area in front and to the sides of the goal area

penalty kick: a kick awarded to the opposing team when the other team commits a foul within its own penalty area

penalty mark: the spot where the ball is placed inside the penalty area for penalty kicks

push pass: a short pass using the inside of the foot

shoelace pass: a powerful pass using the foot's instep

stoppage time: time added to each half of the game by the referee to make up for time lost due to injured players, players being substituted, and so on

striker: center forward whose main job is to score

throw-in: one way the ball is put back into play when it has gone out of bounds

touchlines: the long sidelines of the soccer rectangle

trapping: a way of stopping and controlling the ball with feet, thighs, chest, or head

volley: a kick to an airborne ball

wall pass: a player passes the ball to a teammate, runs around the defense, and then has the ball passed back to him or her

Metric Conversion
1 yard = .9144 meters

Other Words to Know

Here are definitions of some of the words used in this book:

awarded: given to someone

contact: touching something

dominate: to control because of strength and power

flexible: bends easily

interfering: getting in the way of an opponent

latex: a rubbery material that stretches

opponent: the other team, or a player on the other team

professional: a person paid to do a job or play a game

rectangular: in the shape of a rectangle, which is a four-sided object

repeatedly: over and over again

resume: to start up again

skill: being able to do something

unpredictable: when no one can be sure what's going to happen

vary: having many different types

violation: breaking a rule

violence: using force to injure another

Where To Learn More

AT THE LIBRARY

Clark, Brooks and Tommy Stokes. *Kids' Book of Soccer: Skills, Strategies, and the Rules of the Game.* New York: Carol Publishing Group, 1997.

Crisfield, Deborah W. *The Everything Kids' Soccer Book: Rules, Techniques, and More about Your Favorite Sport.* Avon, Mass.: Adams Media Corporation, 2002.

Jones, Cobi, Andrew Gutelle and Paul Meisel. *Cobi Jones Soccer Games.* New York: Workman Publishing Company, Inc., 1998.

ON THE ROAD

American Youth Soccer Organization
12501 South Isis Ave.
Hawthorne, CA 90250
800/872-2976
http://www.soccer.org

National Soccer Hall of Fame
18 Stadium Circle
Oneonta, NY 13820
607/432-3351
http://www.soccerhall.org

ON THE WEB

Federation Internationale de Football Association
http://www.fifa.com

Major League Soccer
http://www.mlsnet.com

U.S. Soccer
http://www.ussoccer.com

U.S. Youth Soccer Association
http://www.usyouthsoccer.org

Women's United Soccer Association
http://www.wusa.com

INDEX

ABOUT THE AUTHOR

Kenn Goin is a New York City writer and editor specializing in books for kids. He has worked for Macmillan, Golden Books, Scholastic, American Greetings and other publishers. While he usually writes about animals and science, he decided to pen this title to honor the long line of sports fans that he grew up with in Texas and New Mexico.